THE COVENANT
OF GRACE

A BIBLICO-THEOLOGICAL STUDY

JOHN MURRAY

Presbyterian and Reformed Publishing Company
Phillipsburg, New Jersey

Manufactured in the United States of America

Library of Congress Cataloging-in-Publication Data

Murray, John, 1898–1975.
   The covenant of grace.

   Reprint. Originally published: London: Tyndale Press, 1954.
   1. Covenants (Theology) I. Title.
BT155.M82   1987   231.7'6   87-29117
ISBN 0-87552-363-3

THE COVENANT OF GRACE

A BIBLICO-THEOLOGICAL STUDY

INTRODUCTION

STUDENTS of historical theology, even those who entertain a radically different view of the history of divine revelation from that which governs the thought of classic Reformed theology, have recognized that the covenant theology marked an epoch in the appreciation and understanding of the progressiveness of divine revelation. William Robertson Smith, for example, gives the following appraisal: ' With all its defects, the Federal theology of Cocceius is the most important attempt, in the older Protestant theology, to do justice to the historical development of revelation '.[1] Geerhardus Vos, steeped in and sympathetic towards the covenant theology, says that it ' has from the beginning shown itself possessed of a true historic sense in the apprehension of the progressive character of the deliverance of truth.'[2]

When we use the term ' covenant theology ', however, we must not restrict this evaluation to the more fully developed covenant theology of the seventeenth century. For in John Calvin there is a distinct emphasis upon the historic progressiveness and continuity of redemptive revelation. We need only to be reminded of the *Institutes,* Book II, Chapters x and xi where he unfolds in detail the similarities and differences of the two Testaments. It is in connection with this discussion that he says: ' The covenant of all the fathers is so far from differing substantially from ours, that it is the very same. Only the administration varies.'[3] Later, in one of the most significant statements relevant to this subject, he says: ' If the subject still appears involved in any obscurity, let us proceed to the very form of the covenant; which will not only satisfy sober minds, but will abundantly prove the ignorance of those who endeavour to oppose it. For the Lord has always covenanted thus with his servants: " I will

---

[1] *The Prophets of Israel,* New York, 1882, p. 375; *cf.* W. Adams Brown: ' Covenant Theology ' in *Encyclopædia of Religion and Ethics,* ed. James Hastings, New York, 1928, vol. IV, p. 218.

[2] ' Hebrews, the Epistle of the Diatheke ' in *The Princeton Theological Review,* vol. XIV, p. 60.

[3] *Inst.* II, x. 2.

be to you a God, and ye shall be to me a people " (Lv. xxvi. 12). These expressions, according to the common explanation of the prophets, comprehend life, and salvation, and consummate felicity.'[4] Nothing could be more pertinent to the perspective which is indispensable to the proper understanding of covenant revelation than the recognition that the central element of the blessing involved in covenant grace is the relationship expressed in the words, ' I will be your God, and ye shall be my people '.

The covenant theology not only recognized the organic unity and progressiveness of redemptive revelation but also the fact that redemptive revelation was covenant revelation and that the religion or piety which was the fruit and goal of this covenant revelation was covenant religion or piety. The necessity of this conclusion can readily be shown by the fact that the relation of grace and promise established by God with Abraham was a covenant relation. It is this Abrahamic covenant, so explicitly set forth in Gn. xv and xvii, that underlies the whole subsequent development of God's redemptive promise, word, and action. It is in terms of the promise given to Abraham, that in him and in his seed all the families of the earth would be blessed,[5] that God sent forth His Son in the fulness of time in order that He might redeem them that were under the law and all without distinction might receive the adoption of sons. It is in fulfilment of this promise to Abraham that there is now no longer Jew nor Gentile, male nor female, bond nor free, that Christ is all and in all, and that all believers are blessed with faithful Abraham.[6] The redemptive grace of God in the highest and furthest reaches of its realization is the unfolding of the promise given to Abraham and therefore the unfolding of the Abrahamic covenant. Soteriology is covenant soteriology and eschatology is covenant eschatology.

The covenant theology was governed by this insight and by this conception. It was in the Reformed theology that the covenant theology developed, and the greatest contribution of covenant theology was its covenant soteriology and eschatology.

It would not be, however, in the interests of theological conservation or theological progress for us to think that the covenant theology is in all respects definitive and that there is no further

[4] *Inst.* II, x. 8.
[5] Gn. xii. 3, xxii. 18, xxvi. 4; Gal. iii. 8, 9, 16.
[6] Rom. iv. 16-18; Gal. iii. 7.

need for correction, modification, and expansion. Theology must always be undergoing reformation. The human understanding is imperfect. However architectonic may be the systematic constructions of any one generation or group of generations, there always remains the need for correction and reconstruction so that the structure may be brought into closer approximation to the Scripture and the reproduction be a more faithful transcript or reflection of the heavenly exemplar. It appears to me that the covenant theology, notwithstanding the finesse of analysis with which it was worked out and the grandeur of its articulated systematization, needs recasting. We would not presume to claim that we shall be so successful in this task that the reconstruction will displace and supersede the work of the classic covenant theologians. But with their help we may be able to contribute a little towards a more biblically articulated and formulated construction of the covenant concept and of its application to our faith, love, and hope.

DEFINITION OF THE TERM ' COVENANT '

From early times in the era of the Reformation and throughout the development of the covenant theology the formulation has been deeply affected by the idea that a covenant is a compact or agreement between two parties. As early as Henry Bullinger's *De Testamento seu Foedere Dei* we find such statements as the following. ' A διαθήκη in the singular number signifies a pact and agreement and promise.'[7] And Bullinger proceeds to construe the covenant of grace as a uniting together of God and man in terms of certain prescriptions — on God's side promises, on man's side the condition of keeping the covenant by fearing the Lord, walking in His ways, and serving Him with the whole heart. Ursinus, in like manner, says: ' A covenant in general signifieth a mutual contract or agreement of two parties joined in the covenant, whereby is made a bond or obligation on certain conditions for the performance of giving or taking something, with addition of outward signs and tokens, for solemn testimony and confirmation that the compact and promise shall be kept inviolable '.[8] Hence God's covenant is

---

[7] *De Testamento seu Foedere Dei Unico et Aeterno.*

[8] *The Summe of Christian Religion* translated by D. Henrie Parry (Oxford, 1601), p. 218.

' a mutual promise and agreement between God and men, whereby God giveth men assurance, that he will be gracious and
favorable to them . . . and on the other side men bind themselves to faith and repentance '.[9] This mutual compact, Ursinus
holds, is sealed by the sacraments, testifying God's will toward
us and our dutifulness toward Him.   John Preston, likewise,
defines a covenant as a compact, agreement, mutual engagement.
The covenant with Abraham comprised four things: (1) the seed
promised and fulfilled in Christ; (2) the condition — faith in the
promise; (3) the confirmation — promise and oath; (4) the parts
which answer to the three offices of Christ.[10]   And William
Perkins says that the covenant of grace is nothing more than ' a
compact made between God and man touching reconciliation
and life everlasting by Christ '.   The parties reconciled are God
and man, God being the principal, promising righteousness and
life in Christ, and man binding himself to faith.   Christ is the
mediator in whom all the promises are yea and amen.[11]

The more scholastic and systematic theologians took their
point of departure from this type of definition.   Peter Van
Mastricht, for example, says that a covenant denotes an agreement (consensus) between God and His people in which God
promises beatitude and stipulates obedience.   Van Mastricht
applies this notion of agreement or consent of parties in different
ways to different covenants and thus makes important distinctions.[12]   But these distinctions are not our concern at present.
Cocceius also construes the covenant of grace as ' an agreement
between God and man a sinner '.[13]

Francis Turretine defines the covenant of grace as ' a gratuitous
pact between God offended and man the offender, entered into
in Christ, in which God promises to man freely on account of

[9] *Ibid.*, p. 219; *cf.* H. à Diest: *Mellificium Catecheticum Continens
Epitomen Catecheticarum Explicationum Ursino-Pareanarum* (Deven-
ter, 1640), p. 89.
[10] *The New Covenant or the Saints Portion* (London, 1639), pp. 313,
347ff.
[11] *An Exposition of the Symbole or Creed of the Apostles, Works,* Vol. I
(London, 1612), pp. 164ff.
[12] *Theoretico-Practica Theologia* (Utrecht, 1698), Lib. III, Cap. XII,
§ VII; Lib. V, Cap. I, §§ VI-XV.
[13] *Summa Doctrinae de Foedere et Testamento Dei,* Cap. IV, § 76,
Summa Theologiae (Amsterdam, 1701), Tome VII, p. 57.

Christ remission of sins and salvation, and man relying on the same grace promises faith and obedience. Or it is a gratuitous agreement between God the offended one and man the offender concerning grace and glory in Christ to be conferred upon man the sinner on the condition of faith '.[14] Consequently the elements in the covenant consist in (1) the Author, (2) the Parties contracting, (3) the Mediator, and (4) the Clauses *a parte Dei* and *a parte hominis*.

Herman Witsius, to take another example, says that ' the covenant of grace is an agreement between God and the elect sinner; God declaring his free goodwill concerning eternal salvation, and everything relative thereto, freely to be given to those in covenant by and for the sake of the Mediator Christ; and man consenting to that goodwill by a sincere faith '.[15]

[14] *Institutio Theologiae Elencticae*, Loc. XI, Quaest. II, § V.
[15] *De Oeconomia Foederum Dei cum Hominibus*, Lib. II, Cap. I, § V. Cf. also Charles Hodge: *Systematic Theology*, Vol. II, pp. 354ff.; W. G. T. Shedd: *Dogmatic Theology* (New York, 1888), Vol. II, pp. 358ff.; R. L. Dabney: *Systematic and Polemic Theology* (Richmond, 1927), pp. 430ff.

There has been, however, a recognition on the part of more recent students of covenant theology that the idea of pact or compact or contract is not adequate or proper as the definition of *berith* and *diatheke* and admirable service has been rendered by such scholars in the analysis and formulation of the biblical concept. *Cf.* Geerhardus Vos: ' Hebrews, the Epistle of the Diatheke ' in *The Princeton Theological Review*, October 1915 and January 1916 (Vol. XIII, pp. 587-632 and Vol. XIV, pp. 1-61); Herman Bavinck: *Gereformeerde Dogmatiek* (Kampen, 1918), Vol. III, pp. 209ff.; G. Ch. Aalders: *Het Verbond Gods* (Kampen, 1939). John Kelly in *The Divine Covenants: their Nature and Design* (London, 1861) says quite dogmatically with reference to *diatheke*: ' It does not properly signify a compact or agreement; there is another Greek word for this, never used for covenant ' (p. 8); *cf.* also David Russell: *A Familiar Survey of the Old and New Covenants* (Edinburgh, 1824), p. 154. Most recently Herman N. Ridderbos: *The Epistle of Paul to the Churches of Galatia* (Grand Rapids, 1953) says: ' In LXX διαθήκη is regularly used as the translation of the covenant of God (*berith*), rather than the apparently more available word συνθήκη. In this there is already an expression of the fact that the covenant of God does not have the character of a contract between two parties, but rather that of a one-sided grant. This corresponds with the covenant-idea in the Old Testament, in which *berith*, even in human relations, sometimes refers

THE USE OF THE TERM IN SCRIPTURE

As we study the biblical evidence bearing upon the nature of divine covenant we shall discover that the emphasis in these theologians upon God's *grace* and *promise* is one thoroughly in accord with the relevant biblical data.   As we shall see, the gracious, promissory character of covenant cannot be over-accented. But the question that confronts us is whether the notion of mutual compact or agreement or convention provides the proper point of departure for our construction of the covenant of grace.   The question now is not whether the theologians who made use of this concept were entirely governed by its implications and carried it out so rigidly in their construction of the covenant of grace that the total result was warped and distorted by the importation and application of this idea.   Furthermore, the question is not whether the idea of compact may not with propriety be used in the interpretation and construction of certain aspects of those divine provisions which lie behind and come to expression in God's administration of saving grace to fallen men. And, finally, the question is not whether mutuality must be ruled out of our conception of what is involved in the relation which the covenant of grace constitutes. The question is simply whether biblico-theological study will disclose that, in the usage of Scripture, covenant (*berith* in Hebrew and *diatheke* in Greek) may properly be interpreted in terms of a mutual pact or agreement.

(a)　*Covenants between men*

When we examine the Scripture we do find that *berith* is applied to relationships established between men.　Abraham and Abimelech made a covenant at Beer-sheba (Gn. xxi. 27, 32).[16] Abimelech said to Isaac, ' Let us make a covenant with thee ' (Gn. xxvi. 28).　Laban said to Jacob, ' Now therefore come thou, and let us make a covenant, I and thou; and let it be for a witness between me and thee ' (Gn. xxxi. 44).　The Gibeonites said to Joshua, ' Make ye a covenant with us ' (Jos. ix. 6, 11, R.V., *cf.*

to a one-party guarantee which a more favored person gives a less favored one (*cf.* Josh. 9: 6, 15, 1 Sam. 11: 1, Ezek. 17: 13). And it is most peculiarly true of the divine covenantal deed that it is a one-party guarantee.   It comes not from man at all, but from God alone ' (p. 130 n.).

[16] The terms used here for making a covenant are כרת ברית. What the significance of כרת is will be reflected on later.

verse 15). David made a covenant with Jonathan, and Jonathan with David (1 Sa. xviii. 3). David made a covenant with Abner (2 Sa. iii. 12, 13, 21); he also made a covenant with all the elders of Israel in Hebron when he became king over all Israel (2 Sa. v. 3). Solomon and Hiram made a covenant (1 Ki. v. 12). It might seem that here undoubtedly the notion of agreement or contract prevails and that to make a covenant is simply to enter into a mutual compact or league.

It must be said, first of all, that, even should it be true that in these covenants the idea of mutual compact is central, it does not follow that the idea of compact is central in or essential to the covenant relation which God constitutes with man. We have to recognize a parity existing between men which cannot obtain in the relation between God and man. And we must also appreciate the flexibility that attaches to the use of terms in Scripture as well as in other literature. Hence we might find that mutual compact is of the essence of covenant when a merely human relationship is in view and that such an idea would be entirely out of place when a divine-human relationship is contemplated.

In the second place, it needs to be noted that the LXX in these cases renders the Hebrew *berith* by the Greek word *diatheke*. This is significant because, if mutual compact belonged to the essence of covenant in these cases, we should have expected the translators to use *suntheke*. To say the least this raises our suspicion that the LXX translators were not governed by the thought of mutual agreement when they came to these instances of covenantal human relationships. Geerhardus Vos is mistaken when he says that ' where the *berith* is made between man and man and consists in a mutual agreement, the translators do not employ διαθήκη but συνθήκη , a word exactly corresponding to the word covenant '.[17] The term *suntheke* hardly ever appears in the canonical books of the LXX. It appears two or three times but only once *possibly* as the translation of *berith*.[18] In

---

17 ' Hebrews, the Epistle of the Diatheke ' in *The Princeton Theological Review*, Vol. XIII, p. 603.

18 2 Ki. xvii. 15. Other instances of συνθήκη are Is. xxviii. 15, where it is not at all likely that it is the translation of בְּרִית but rather of חֹזֶה, and Is. xxx. 1, where it is the translation of מַסֵּכָה. It appears several times in the apocryphal books. Aquila and Symmachus have συνθήκη frequently and Theodotion a few times.

this one possible case it refers to the Lord's covenant with Israel.

In the third place, when we examine some of the instances in question we shall discover that the thought of pact or contract is not in the foreground. It is not denied that there is engagement or commitment in reference to something upon which the person entering into covenant is agreed. Abimelech said to Isaac, 'Let us make a covenant with thee; that thou wilt do us no hurt, as we have not touched thee' (Gn. xxvi. 28, 29). And Laban said to Jacob, 'Let us make a covenant, I and thou; and let it be for a witness between me and thee' (Gn. xxxi. 44). And Laban and Jacob apparently agreed that they would not pass over the heap and pillar to each other for harm (*cf.* verse 52). There is engagement or commitment indeed. But when all the instances of merely human covenants are examined, it would definitely appear that the notion of sworn fidelity is thrust into prominence in these covenants rather than that of mutual contract. It is not the contractual terms that are in prominence so much as the solemn engagement of one person to another. To such an extent is this the case that stipulated terms of agreement need not be present at all. It is the giving of oneself over in the commitment of troth that is emphasized and the specified conditions as those upon which the engagement or commitment is contingent are not mentioned. It is the promise of unreserved fidelity, of whole-souled commitment that appears to constitute the essence of the covenant. There is promise, there may be the sealing of that promise by oath, and there is the bond resultant upon these elements. It is a bonded relationship of unreserved commitment in respect of the particular thing involved or the relationship constituted. This is well illustrated by what David says to Jonathan: 'thou hast brought thy servant into a covenant of the Lord with thee' (1 Sa. xx. 8). David accords to Jonathan's commitment the bonded character of divine sanction and regards it as sealed by divine oath.

If this analysis of the nature of these human covenants is correct, then the idea of stipulations and conditions devised by mutual consultation and agreed upon as the terms of engagement need not to be present even in human covenants. There is, of course, the bond of commitment to one another, but so profound and all-embracing is this commitment that the notion of contractual stipulations recedes into the background or disappears entirely. To say the least, the case is such in these instances of human relationship that no evidence can be derived from them to support the idea of mutual contract or compact.

(b)　Covenants made by man with God

The next type of covenant to be considered is the covenant of human initiative entered into with the Lord. In the days of Joshua the people said, ' The Lord our God will we serve, and unto his voice will we hearken ' (Jos. xxiv. 24, R.V.), and in answer to this promise ' Joshua made a covenant with the people that day, and set them a statute and an ordinance in Shechem ' (xxiv. 25). There is the case of Jehoiada who ' made a covenant between the Lord and the king and the people, that they should be the Lord's people ' (2 Ki. xi. 17). Josiah ' made a covenant before the Lord, to walk after the Lord, and to keep his commandments, and his testimonies, and his statutes, with all his heart, and all his soul, to confirm the words of this covenant that were written in this book: and all the people stood to the covenant ' (2 Ki. xxiii. 3, R.V.). Finally, Ezra said to the people in his day, ' Now therefore let us make a covenant with our God to put away all the wives ' (Ezr. x. 3). These are instances of covenanting with God. We cannot fail to note that what is in the forefront in these cases is not a contract or compact. Strictly speaking, it is not an agreement. Though the persons entering into covenant agree to do certain things, the precise thought is not that of agreement by the people among themselves, nor a mutual agreement between the people and the Lord. We must distinguish between devising terms of agreement or striking an agreement, on the one hand, and the agreement of consent or commitment, on the other What we find in these instances is solemn, promissory commitment to faith or troth on the part of the people concerned. They bind themselves in bond to be faithful to the Lord in accordance with His revealed will. The covenant is solemn pledging of devotion to God, unreserved and unconditional commitment to His service. We are far away from the idea of a bond as sealed on the acceptance of certain prescribed stipulations and the promise of fulfilment of these stipulations on the condition that other parties to the contract fulfil the conditions imposed upon them. The thought is rather that of unreserved, whole-souled commitment.

(c) *Divine covenants*

When we pass on to those instances of covenant which are speci-fically divine it is here that the question becomes particularly pointed and urgent: does the idea of mutual compact or agree-ment constitute the essence of a divine covenant? Or, if this points the question too sharply, is mutual compact or agreement an integral element in the biblical conception of a covenant which God dispenses to men?

There are a few instances in the Old Testament where the word covenant is used with reference to God's creative and providential ordinances. The covenant of the day and of the night is synonymous with the ordinances of day and night (Je. xxxiii. 20, 25). Obviously what is emphasized is the stability and perpetuity of these ordinances arising from the ordination of God and the immutability arising from such ordination. There may also be an allusion to the promise given after the flood that while the earth remained seedtime and harvest, cold and heat, summer and winter, day and night would not cease (Gn. viii. 22). In that event the faithfulness of God not only to His providential ordinances but also to His promise would be brought into view, and the total thought would be that covenant in this connection points to the ordinances of God as immovably established by the ordination, power, and faithfulness of God. We are given some indication of the way in which covenant may be used to express divine monergism and fidelity.

THE POST-DILUVIAN NOAHIC COVENANT

We come now to those instances of covenant administration which have respect to God's bestowal of grace upon men, instances with which we are directly concerned in our attempt to discover what precisely constitutes a covenant and what pre-cisely is the nature of that relation on the part of God to men which covenant constitution contemplates. We may consider, first of all, that instance which, perhaps more than any other in Scripture, assists us in discovering what the essence of covenant is, namely, the post-diluvian Noahic covenant (Gn. ix. 9-17). In regard to this covenant the following features are patent.

1. It is God's covenant in that it is conceived, devised, deter-mined, established, confirmed, and dispensed by God Himself. ' And I, behold I, am establishing my covenant with you ' (Gn.

ix. 9; *cf.* verses 11, 12, 13, 17).

2.   It is universal in its scope, a covenant not only with Noah
but with his seed after him and with every living creature (verses
9, 10).   This places in obvious relief the fact that it affects for
good even those who do not have any intelligent understanding
of its meaning.   The covenant operates for good to such an
extent that its benefits are not contingent upon intelligent appreciation of the covenant or of the benefits which are dispensed in
terms of it.

We must not forget, of course, that the blessings bestowed in
terms of this covenant are not dispensed in complete abstraction
from the revelation given at the time of its establishment nor in
abstraction from understanding of its significance on the part of
men.   God spoke to Noah and to his sons.   This was revelation,
and revelation implies subjects endowed with the intellectual
capacity to understand its character and its effects.   Furthermore,
we may not forget that the covenant purpose and grace were
made known to Noah, and the perpetuity of the covenant is con-
tinuously attested in order that those capable of understanding
may have confidence in the security and perpetuity of the covenant grace bestowed.   But we must also observe that the covenant
operates on behalf of, and dispenses its blessings to, those who
are wholly unaware of its existence.   It is a covenant with all
flesh.

3.   It is an unconditional covenant.   This feature is, of course,
co-ordinate with the fact that intelligent understanding is not
indispensable to the reception of its benefits.   But the particular
consideration now in view is that no commandment is appended
which could be construed as the condition upon which the
promise is to be fulfilled.   And there is not the slightest sugges-
tion to the effect that the covenant could be annulled by human
unfaithfulness or its blessing forfeited by unbelief; the thought of
breaking the covenant is inconceivable.   The confirmation given
is to the opposite effect.   In a word, the promise is unconditional.

4.   The covenant is intensely and pervasively monergistic.
Nothing exhibits this more clearly than the fact that the sign
attached to attest and seal the divine faithfulness and the
irrevocability of God's promise is one produced by conditions
over which God alone has control and in connection with which
there is rigid exclusion of human co-operation.   The sign is not
an action instituted by God and performed by man at the divine

behest. It is one in which there is no human agency whatsoever. Even what is *said* regarding the bow in the cloud has a Godward reference. God will see it to remember the everlasting covenant. There is, doubtless, anthropomorphism here. But it is anthropomorphism for the purpose of bringing to the forefront the unilateral character of the covenant. It is true that the revelatory purpose of the bow in the cloud is not to be forgotten. But the significant fact is that the revelatory purpose is to bear witness to the divine faithfulness. It is the constant reminder that God will not prove unfaithful to His promise. The main point to be stressed now, however, is that this continuance is dependent upon divine faithfulness alone; in anthropomorphic terms, upon the divine remembrance alone. And if we fail to interpret the sign aright, if we regard it simply as a natural phenomenon without any reference to its covenantal meaning, this does not negate or nullify the divine remembrance and the perpetuity of God's faithfulness. ' I will look upon it, that I may remember the everlasting covenant between God and every living creature of all flesh that is upon the earth ' (Gn. ix. 16).

5. It is an everlasting covenant. All flesh will not again be cut off by the waters of the flood (Gn. ix. 11). The perpetuity is bound up with its divinely unilateral and monergistic character. It is because it is divine in its origin, administration, establishment, and confirmation that it can be perpetual. And we may say that the perpetuity both stems from and witnesses to its divinity. Perpetuity and divinity are complementary and mutually interdependent.

These features of the covenant plainly evince that this covenant is a sovereign, divine administration, that it is such in its conception, determination, disclosure, confirmation, and fulfilment, that it is an administration or dispensation of forbearance and goodness, that it is not conditioned by or dependent upon faith or obedience on the part of men. It is an administration of grace which emanates from the sovereign good pleasure of God and continues without any modification or retraction of its benefits by the immutable promise and faithfulness of God.

It is quite apparent that in this covenant we must not take our point of departure from the idea of compact, or contract, or agreement in any respect whatsoever. It is not contractual in its origin, or in its constitution, or in its operation, or in its outcome. Its fulfilment or continuance is not in the least degree contingent even upon reciprocal obligation or appreciation on the part of its beneficiaries. Yet it is a covenant made with men, with Noah and his sons and their seed after them to perpetual generations. It is a covenant characterized by divinity in a way unsurpassed by any other covenant and yet it draws men within the scope of its operation as surely as any other covenant does. Here we have covenant in the purity of its conception as a dispensation of grace to men, wholly divine in its origin, fulfilment, and confirmation.

The question inevitably faces us: may we consider the post-diluvian Noahic covenant as providing us with the essential features of a divine covenant with men? Is there not in this covenant that which makes it inappropriate as the criterion of the terms which could govern the covenant relationship of God with men on the highest level? In this covenant creation as a whole is brought within the scope of the favour bestowed. Hence it can be argued that the relationship with men involved in this covenant must be on a denominator that is common to man and to the non-moral creation and cannot, therefore, possess any of the differentiating features which would characterize covenant relationship to men as men. Needless to say this consideration must be taken into account in our interpretation of what constitutes divine covenant on the highest level of blessing and relationship. And yet it would be unwarranted to disregard entirely the direction of thought provided by this particular covenant.

An aspect of this differentiation appears in the pre-diluvian Noahic covenant, the first instance of reference to covenant in the Old Testament (see Gn. vi. 18). In this case Noah was commanded to do certain things and the doing of these things on the part of Noah was the indispensable condition of the fulfilment of the grace provided for in the covenant. ' Thus did Noah according to all that God commanded him, so did he ' (Gn. vi. 22). Yet even in this case, where obedience to commandments is the means through which the grace of the covenant is to be realized and enjoyed, we must also take note of the fact that in other respects this covenant exhibits the features of divine initiation, determination, establishment, and confirmation which are so conspicuous in the post-diluvian Noahic covenant. The idea of compact or agreement is just as conspicuously absent as in the post-diluvian.

Significantly enough, the commandments which are appended, compliance with which on the part of Noah is indispensable to the blessing of preservation, do not in the least suggest mutuality of agreement or compact. The commandments are added in such a way that they are just as sovereign and unilateral in prescription or dispensation as is the annunciation of the covenant itself. The appended requirements are simply extensions, applications, expressions of the grace intimated in the covenant. The directions are as sovereign as the annunciation of the covenant and they flow naturally from it so that there is no deflection from the idea of sovereign dispensation. We may think of Noah as co-operating with God in carrying out the provisions of the covenant but the co-operation is quite foreign to that of pact or convention. It is the co-operation of response which the grace of the covenant constrains and demands.

THE ABRAHAMIC COVENANT

When we come to the Abrahamic covenant we find features which are entirely new in connection with covenant administration. The first distinctive feature appears in connection with the initial reference to the covenant (Gn. xv. 8-18). It is the solemn sanction by which the Lord confirmed to Abraham the certainty of the promise that he would inherit the land of Canaan. It is perhaps the most striking sanction that we have in the whole of Scripture, particularly if we interpret it as a self-maledictory oath[19] in which, anthropomorphically, God calls upon Himself the curse of dismemberment if He does not fulfil to Abraham the promise of possessing the land. The second distinctive feature is the refer-

---

[19] *Cf.* Je. xxxiv. 18-20. It has been widely held that the expression כרת ברית, which is the standard one for making a covenant, is derived from the cutting asunder of the animals and the ceremony connected with it by which covenants were confirmed. On this assumption the terminology is derived from the solemn sanction by which a covenant was sealed. Gn. xv. 8-18; Je. xxxiv. 18-20 would appear to lend support to this view (*cf.* Ps. l. 5). While there does not seem to be any other satisfactory explanation of the expression כרת ברית, yet there is not sufficient evidence for a conclusive judgment in favour of this widely-held interpretation. We shall probably have to wait for light which may yet be derived from other sources.

ence to keeping and breaking the covenant (Gn. xvii. 9, 10, 14).[20]

With reference to the first distinctive feature there are certain observations which are pertinent to the question we are now pursuing.

(1) Though this feature is signally distinctive, it underlines what we have found already respecting the earlier covenants, namely, that a covenant is a divine administration, divine in its origin, establishment, confirmation and fulfilment. It is not Abraham who passes through between the divided pieces of the animals; it is the theophany. And the theophany represents God. The action therefore is divinely unilateral. It is confirmation to Abraham, not confirmation from him. Abraham here does not pledge his troth to God by a self-maledictory oath but God condescends to pledge troth to his promise, a fact which advertises the divine sovereignty and faithfulness as brought to bear upon and as giving character to the covenant constituted. ' In the same day the Lord made a covenant with Abram, saying, Unto thy seed have I given this land, from the river of Egypt unto the great river, the river Euphrates ' (Gn. xv. 18).

(2) The distinctiveness of the sanction and the added solemnity which it involves are correlative with the intimacy and spirituality of the blessing which the covenant imparts. The essence of the blessing is that God will be the God of Abraham and of his seed, the characteristic promise of the Old Testament, ' I will be your God, and ye shall be my people '. In a word, this consists in union and communion with the Lord.

With reference to the second distinctive feature, namely, the necessity of keeping the covenant and the warning against breaking it, we cannot suppress the inference that the necessity of keeping is complementary to the added richness, intimacy, and spirituality of the covenant itself. The spirituality of the Abrahamic covenant in contrast with the Noahic consists in the fact that the Abrahamic is concerned with religious relationship on the highest level, union and communion with God. Where there is religious relationship there is mutuality and where we

---

[20] The verb used in verse 14 for breaking is פרר. Various other terms are used elsewhere in the Old Testament to express this same notion, such as transgress (עבר —Dt. xvii. 2), forsake (עזב —Dt. xxix. 24), unstedfast in (לא אמן — Ps. lxxviii. 37). The Old Testament likewise speaks of the quarrel of the covenant (Lv. xxvi. 25) and the curses of the covenant (Dt. xxix. 20).

have religious relationship on the highest conceivable level there. mutuality on the highest plane of spirituality must obtain. This is just saying that there must be response on the part of the beneficiary and response on the highest level of religious devotion. The keeping of the covenant, therefore, so far from being incompatible with the nature of the covenant as an administration of grace, divine in its initiation, confirmation, and fulfilment, is a necessity arising from the intimacy and spirituality of the religious relation involved. The more enhanced our conception of the sovereign grace bestowed the more we are required to posit reciprocal faithfulness on the part of the recipient. The demands of appreciation and gratitude increase with the length and breadth and depth and height of the favour bestowed. And such demands take concrete practical form in the obligation to obey the commandments of God.

We are led to the conclusion that in the Abrahamic covenant there is no deviation from the idea of covenant as a sovereign dispensation of grace. We have found that grace is intensified and expanded rather than diminished and the greater the grace the more accentuated becomes the sovereignty of its administration. The necessity of keeping the covenant on the part of men does not interfere with the divine monergism of dispensation. The necessity of keeping is but the expression of the magnitude of the grace bestowed and the spirituality of the relation constituted. Even in this case the notion of compact or agreement is alien to the nature of the covenant constitution.

It may plausibly be objected, however, that the breaking of the covenant envisaged in this case interferes with the perpetuity of the covenant. For does not the possibility of breaking the covenant imply conditional perpetuity? ' The uncircumcised male . . . shall be cut off from his people; he hath broken my covenant ' (Gn. xvii. 14, R.V.). Without question the blessings of the covenant and the relation which the covenant entails cannot be enjoyed or maintained apart from the fulfilment of certain conditions on the part of the beneficiaries. For when we think of the promise which is the central element of the covenant, ' I will be your God, and ye shall be my people ', there is necessarily involved, as we have seen, mutuality in the highest sense. Fellowship is always mutual and when mutuality ceases fellowship ceases. Hence the reciprocal response of faith and obedience arises from the nature of the relationship which the covenant contemplates (*cf*. Gn xviii. 17-19; xxii. 16-18). The obedience of Abraham is represented as the condition upon which the fulfilment of the promise given to him was contingent and the obedience of Abraham's seed is represented as the means through which the promise given to Abraham would be accomplished. There is undoubtedly the fulfilment of certain conditions and these are summed up in obeying the Lord's voice and keeping His covenant.

It is not quite congruous, however, to speak of these conditions as conditions of the covenant. For when we speak thus we are distinctly liable to be understood as implying that the covenant is not to be regarded as dispensed until the conditions are fulfilled and that the conditions are integral to the establishment of the covenant relation. And this would not provide a true or accurate account of the covenant. The covenant is a sovereign dispensation of God's grace. It is grace bestowed and a relation established. The grace dispensed and the relation established do not wait for the fulfilment of certain conditions on the part of those to whom the grace is dispensed. Grace is bestowed and the relation established by sovereign divine administration. How then are we to construe the conditions of which we have spoken? The continued enjoyment of this grace and of the relation established is contingent upon the fulfilment of certain conditions. For apart from the fulfilment of these conditions the grace bestowed and the relation established are meaningless. Grace bestowed implies a subject and reception on the part of that subject. The relation established implies mutuality. But the conditions in view are not really conditions of bestowal. They are simply the reciprocal responses of faith, love and obedience, apart from which the enjoyment of the covenant blessing and of the covenant relation is inconceivable. In a word, keeping the covenant presupposes the covenant relation as established rather than the condition upon which its establishment is contingent.

It is when viewed in this light that the breaking of the covenant takes on an entirely different complexion. It is not the failure to meet the terms of a pact nor failure to respond to the offer of favourable terms of contractual agreement. It is unfaithfulness to a relation constituted and to grace dispensed. By breaking the covenant what is broken is not the condition of bestowal but the condition of consummated fruition.

It should be noted also that the necessity of keeping the covenant is bound up with the particularism of this covenant. The covenant does not yield its blessing to all indiscriminately. The discrimination which this covenant exemplifies accentuates the sovereignty of God in the bestowal of its grace and the fulfilment of its promises. This particularization is correlative with the spirituality of the grace bestowed and the relation constituted and it is also consonant with the exactitude of its demands. A covenant which yields its blessing indiscriminately is not one that can be kept or broken. We see again, therefore, that the intensification which particularism illustrates serves to accentuate the keeping which is indispensable to the fruition of the covenant grace.

THE MOSAIC COVENANT

The Mosaic covenant offers more plausible support to the conception of compact than does any other covenant of God with men. Furthermore, the notion of prescribed conditions would appear to receive more support from the circumstances of this covenant than from those of any other. Such considerations as these have been the occasion for constructions which set the Mosaic covenant in sharp contrast both with the Abrahamic covenant and the New Testament.

At the outset we must remember that the idea of conditional fulfilment is not something peculiar to the Mosaic covenant. We have been faced quite poignantly with this very question in connection with the Abrahamic covenant. And since this feature is there patent, it does not of itself provide us with any reason for construing the Mosaic covenant in terms different from those of the Abrahamic. Another preliminary observation is that the deliverance of the children of Israel from Egypt is stated expressly to be in pursuance of the Abrahamic covenant. With reference to the Egyptian bondage we read: ' And God heard their groaning, and God remembered his covenant with Abraham, with Isaac, and with Jacob ' (Ex. ii. 24). The only interpretation of this is that the deliverance of Israel from Egypt and the bringing of them into the land of promise is in fulfilment of the covenant promise to Abraham respecting the possession of the land of Canaan (Ex. iii. 16, 17, vi. 4-8; Pss. cv. 8-12, 42-45, cvi. 45). A third observation is that the spirituality of relationship which is the centre of the Abrahamic covenant is also at the centre of the Mosaic. ' And I will take you to me for a people, and I will be to you a God ' (Ex. vi. 7; *cf.* Dt. xxix. 13). This fact links the Mosaic very closely with the Abrahamic and shows that religious relationship on the highest level is contemplated in both, namely, union and communion with God. We must not, therefore, suppress or discount these important considerations that the Mosaic covenant was made with Israel as the *sequel* to their deliverance from Egypt, a deliverance wrought in pursuance of the gracious promises given by covenant to Abraham, wrought with the object of bringing to fulfilment the promise given to Abraham that his seed would inherit the land of Canaan, and a deliverance wrought in order to make Israel His own peculiar and adopted people.

The first express reference to the covenant made with Israel at Sinai occurs in connection with keeping the covenant. ' Now therefore, if ye will obey my voice indeed, and keep my covenant, then ye shall be a peculiar treasure unto me above all people: for all the earth is mine. And ye shall be unto me a kingdom of priests, and an holy nation ' (Ex. xix. 5, 6). The next explicit reference appears as the sequel to the promise of the people, ' All that the Lord hath spoken will we do, and be obedient ' (Ex. xxiv. 7, R.V.) and Moses sprinkled the blood and said, ' Behold, the blood of the covenant, which the Lord hath made with you concerning all these words ' (Ex. xxiv. 8).

The foregoing references as well as other considerations might create the impression that the making of the covenant had to wait for the voluntary acceptance on the part of the people and their promise to obey and keep it. A close study of these passages will not bear out such an interpretation. It is an importation contrary to the texts themselves and one that has deflected the course of thought on this subject. Ex. xix. 5 does not say, ' If ye will obey my voice and accept the terms stipulated, then I will make my covenant with you '. What is said is, ' If ye will obey my voice indeed, and keep my covenant, then ye shall be a peculiar treasure unto me '. The covenant is conceived of as dispensed, as in operation, and as constituting a certain relation, in the keeping of it and in obeying God's voice. The covenant is actually presupposed in the keeping of it. Undoubtedly there is a conditional feature to the words, ' If ye will obey my voice indeed, and keep my covenant '. But what is conditioned upon obedience and keeping of the covenant is the enjoyment of the blessing which the covenant contemplates. In like manner in Ex. xxiv. 7, 8, the covenant is not to be regarded as contingent upon the promise of the people, so that the dispensing of the covenant had to wait for this promise. And verse 8 is not to be construed as if then the covenant had been inaugurated or as if acceptance on the part of the people completed the process of constituting the covenant relation. The covenant had already been established and the blood was simply the confirmation or seal of the covenant established and of the relation constituted. This gives a different perspective to our interpretation of the Mosaic covenant, and we find that the Mosaic covenant also is a sovereign administration of grace, divinely initiated, established, confirmed, and fulfilled. Later references in the Pentateuch confirm this interpretation of sovereign appointment or dispensation (Ex. xxxiv. 27, 28; Lv. xxiv. 8; Nu. xviii. 19, xxv. 13; cf. Ne. xiii. 29).

The question of the condition referred to above does call, however, for some consideration. How does the condition of obedience comport with the concept of a monergistic administration of grace? The answer must follow the lines which have been delineated above in connection with the keeping of the Abrahamic covenant. What needs to be emphasized now is that the Mosaic covenant in respect of the condition of obedience is not in a different category from the Abrahamic. It is too frequently assumed that the conditions prescribed in connection with the Mosaic covenant place the Mosaic dispensation in a totally different category as respects grace, on the one hand, and demand or obligation, on the other. In reality there is nothing that is principially different in the necessity of keeping the covenant and of obedience to God's voice, which proceeds from the Mosaic covenant, from that which is involved in the keeping required in the Abrahamic. In both cases the keynotes are obeying God's voice and keeping the covenant (cf. Gn. xviii. 17-19; Ex. xix. 5, 6).

The Davidic Covenant

If the Mosaic covenant does not disclose deviation from the fundamental notion of a covenant, namely, that it is a sovereign dispensation, divine in its origin, establishment, confirmation, and fulfilment, we should not expect that subsequent covenant administrations would evince a radically different conception. Indeed so basic to the whole subsequent process of redemptive history are the Abrahamic and Mosaic covenants that the later developments would be expected to confirm and intensify what we have found to be the specific character of covenant administration. Although the word covenant does not occur in 2 Sa. vii. 12-17, we must conclude that this is specifically the annunciation to David which is elsewhere spoken of as the covenant made with David. In Ps. lxxxix. 3, 4 the terms of 2 Sa. vii. 12-17 are clearly reiterated. 'I have made a covenant with my chosen, I have sworn unto David my servant: thy seed will I establish for ever, and build up thy throne to all generations.' And the same is true in later verses of the same Psalm (cf. verses 26ff.). 'My covenant shall stand fast with him' (verse 28). 'My covenant will I not break, nor alter the thing that is gone out of my lips' (verse 34; cf. Ps. cxxxii. 11ff.). A study of these passages will show that the most striking feature is the security, the determinateness, and immutability of the divine promise. Nothing could serve to verify the conception of the covenant which has been elicited from earlier instances more than the emphasis in these passages (relating to the Davidic covenant) upon the certainty of fulfilment arising from the promise and oath of God. Security and certainty as characterizing the covenant could not be more plainly demonstrated than by the parallelism: 'I have made a covenant with my chosen, I have sworn unto David my servant'. And David reflects this note of certainty when, at the close of his career, his resort for consolation and assurance was nothing else than the covenant of his God: 'Verily my house is not so with God; yet he hath made with me an everlasting covenant, ordered in all things, and sure: for it is all my salvation, and all my desire, although he maketh it not to grow' (2 Sa. xxiii. 5). No example of covenant in the Old Testament more clearly supports the thesis that covenant is sovereign promise, promise solemnized by the sanctity of an oath, immutable in its security and divinely confirmed as respects the certainty of its fulfilment.

These Davidic promises are, of course, messianic; it is in Christ that David's seed is established for ever and his throne built up to all generations. In this connection we cannot overlook the relevance of those passages in Isaiah in which the servant of the Lord is said to be given for a covenant of the people. The prophet

introduces this messianic personage with the words, ' Behold, my
servant, whom I uphold; mine elect, in whom my soul delighteth '
(Is. xlii. 1). And he quickly adds: ' I the Lord have called thee
in righteousness, and will hold thine hand, and will keep thee,
and give thee for a covenant of the people, for a light of the
Gentiles ' (verse 6). Later he reiterates: ' And I will preserve
thee, and give thee for a covenant of the people ' (Is. xlix. 8).
The co-ordination of Is. lv. 3, 4 is equally significant: ' Incline
your ear, and come unto me; hear, and your soul shall live; and
I will make an everlasting covenant with you, even the sure
mercies of David. Behold, I have given him for a witness to the
peoples, a leader and commander to the peoples ' (r.v.). Nothing
less than sovereign dispensation and unilateral bestowment will
comport with the donation of the servant as a covenant of the
people. Any notion of agreement or compact would ruthlessly
violate the sovereignty of the grace involved and the divine
monergism of the action entailed. And no doubt this unusual
way of expressing the bestowment of grace is dictated by the consideration that nothing accentuates the certainty and security of
promise and fulfilment more than to invest the assurance given
with the sanction of covenant. Furthermore, in these Isaianic
passages the inference is inevitable that the everlasting covenant
which the Lord makes with the people is correlative with the fact
that He has given the servant as a covenant of the people. The
security of the covenant with the people is grounded in the
security of the donation of the servant as a covenant of the
people. And when Malachi calls the messenger ' the messenger
of the covenant' (Mal. iii. 1), there is the implication that not
only is the Messiah given for a covenant of the people but that
when He is sent forth to discharge His office it is in terms of the
covenant that He does this. He is the angel of the covenant
because He comes in pursuance of the covenant promise and
purpose, and He is Himself the covenant because the blessings
and provisions of the covenant are to such an extent bound up
with Him that He is Himself the embodiment of these blessings
and of the presence of the Lord with His people which the covenant insures. To whatever extent the response of inclining the
ear, of hearing, and of coming (Is. lv. 3) may be requisite in
order that the blessings of covenant grace and relationship may
be ours, it must be apparent that the covenant itself is a sovereign
donation of the child born and the Son given (Is. ix. 6). There

is nothing that corresponds to the contractual in the declaration
' I will give thee for a covenant of the people ' nor in the promise
' I will make an everlasting covenant with you, even the sure
mercies of David '. Elsewhere in this prophecy of Isaiah it is
the certitude and immutability of God's grace that is thrust into
prominence in connection with covenant disclosure. ' This is as
the waters of Noah unto me: for as I have sworn that the waters
of Noah should no more go over the earth; so have I sworn that
I would not be wroth with thee, nor rebuke thee. For the moun-
tains shall depart, and the hills be removed; but my lovingkind-
ness shall not depart from thee, neither shall the covenant of my
peace be removed, saith the Lord that hath mercy on thee ' (Is.
liv. 9, 10; *cf.* lix. 21). This passage shows that the post-diluvian
Noahic covenant provides the pattern or type of what is involved
in God's covenant of peace with His people, namely, that it is
an oath-bound and oath-certified assurance of irrevocable grace
and promise.

COVENANT IN THE NEW TESTAMENT

When we come to the New Testament a goodly number of the
instances of *diatheke* are references to Old Testament covenants,
sometimes in quotation from the Old Testament (Lk. i. 72; Acts
iii. 35, vii. 8; Rom. ix. 4, xi. 27; 2 Cor. iii. 14; Gal. iii. 15, 17,
iv. 24; Eph. ii. 12; Heb. viii. 9, ix. 4, 15, 20). There are others
which refer to Old Testament promises, though not specifically
to Old Testament covenants.

There are instructive lessons, pertinent to our inquiry, to be
derived from these Old Testament allusions. The first (Lk. i.
72) is illumining in this respect. When Zacharias says that the
Lord, the God of Israel, had remembered His holy covenant, the
oath which He had sworn to Abraham, it is apparent that he
construes the redemptive events which form the subject of his
doxology as a fulfilment of the Abrahamic covenant. The
language of his blessing is unmistakably reminiscent of the
language used when God had been preparing His people for the
imminent deliverance from the bondage of Egypt. We cannot
escape the inference that the redemptive accomplishment signal-
ized by the coming of Christ found its historical prototype in
the redemption from Egypt. In Zacharias' esteem it is the same
fidelity to covenant promise and oath that is exemplified in the

accomplishment of redemption through Christ and in the redemption from Egypt by the hand of Moses and Aaron. This indicates that the undergirding principle of the thought of pious Israelites at this time was the unity and continuity of God's covenant revelation and action, a principle which came to spontaneous expression in the thanksgiving of Zacharias and bears the imprimatur of the Holy Spirit. It was by inspiration that Zacharias spoke, for we are told that he ' was filled with the Holy Ghost, and prophesied ' (Lk. i. 67).

Another observation worthy of note is the occurrence of the plural ' covenants ' in reference to the privilege of Israel (Rom. ix. 4; Eph. ii. 12). Apparently the New Testament writers did not think of the peculiar prerogatives of Israel in terms simply of the Abrahamic covenant even though this covenant is given very distinct prominence in other passages. And of more significance is the fact that Paul speaks of these covenants as ' the covenants of promise ' (Eph. ii. 12). He does not hesitate to place the various covenants which constituted the distinctiveness of Israel in the category of promise just as he does not hesitate to list the ' covenants ' together with the adoption and the glory and the giving of the law and the service of God and the promises (Rom. ix. 4). In this we are advised of the direction in which we are to seek for the New Testament conception of covenant.

Most significant of all, perhaps, in this classification of New Testament passages is Gal. iii. 15, 17. Paul's emphasis here is upon the immutability, security, inviolability of covenant. ' Though it be but a man's covenant, yet when it hath been confirmed, no one makes it void, or adds thereto.' ' A covenant confirmed beforehand by God, the law, which came four hundred and thirty years after, does not disannul, so as to make the promise of no effect.' Whatever view we may entertain regarding the precise import of *diatheke* in this passage, whether it is the testamentary or the dispensatory, we cannot escape the governing thought of the apostle, namely, that a human covenant is irrevocable once it has been confirmed and that it is that same inviolability which characterizes the Abrahamic covenant and therefore, also, the promise which the covenant embraced. Here, without question, covenant appears as a promise and dispensation of grace, divinely established, confirmed, and fulfilled, inviolable in its provisions and of permanent validity.

(a) *The new covenant and the old*

When we come to those passages in the New Testament which deal specifically with the new covenant in contrast with the old it is highly significant that the contrast between the new economy and the old is not expressed in terms of difference between covenant and something else not a covenant. The contrast is within the ambit of covenant. This would lead us to expect that the basic idea of covenant which we find in the Old Testament is carried over into the New. We are confirmed in this expectation when we take account of the fact that the new covenant is the fulfilment of the covenant made with Abraham (Lk. i. 72; Gal. iii. 15ff.). The new economy as covenant attaches itself to the Old Testament covenant promise and cannot be contrasted with Old Testament covenant in respect of that which constitutes the essence of covenant grace and promise. We can express the fact that the new covenant is the expansion and fulfilment of the Abrahamic by saying that it was just because the promise to Abraham had the bonded and oath-bound character of a covenant that its realization in the fulness of the time was inviolably certain. The new covenant in respect of its being a covenant does not differ from the Abrahamic as a sovereign administration of grace, divine in its inception, establishment, confirmation, and fulfilment. The most conclusive evidence, however, is derived from a study of the New Testament respecting the nature of the new covenant. We shall find that the features of the covenant are the same as those we found in connection with covenant in the Old Testament.

When our Lord said that His blood was the blood of the covenant that was shed for many for the remission of sins and that the cup of the last supper was the new covenant in His blood (Mt. xxvi. 28; Mk. xiv. 24; Lk. xxii. 20; 1 Cor. xi. 25), we cannot but regard the covenant as a designation of the sum-total of grace, blessing, truth, and relationship comprised in that redemption which His blood has secured. Covenant must refer to the bestowment and the relationship secured by the sacrificial blood which He shed. It is the fulness of grace purchased by His blood and conveyed by it. By way of comparison there is an allusion, no doubt, to the blood by which the old covenant, the Mosaic, had been sealed (Ex. xxiv. 6-8; *cf.* Heb. ix. 18). And since the new is contrasted with the old it cannot be that the contrast inheres in any retraction or dilution of the grace which we have found to be the essence of covenant under the Old Testament.

Apart from the reference to the institution of the Lord's Supper in 1 Cor. xi. 25, the only passage in Paul where he refers expressly to the new covenant is 2 Cor. iii. 6. Here, however, we have the most illumining reflection upon the nature of the new covenant. It is the ministration of the Spirit as the Spirit of life (verses 6, 8). It is the ministration of righteousness (verse 9), and of liberty (verse 17). Most characteristically of all, it is the ministry of that transfiguration by which we are transformed into the image of the Lord Himself.   When we assess the significance of such blessings in terms of New Testament teaching and specifically of Pauline teaching we see that Paul conceives of the new covenant as that which ministers the highest blessing and constitutes the relationship to God which is the crown and goal of the redemptive process and the apex of the religious relationship.

When we turn to the Epistle to the Hebrews and particularly to those passages in which the contrast is drawn between the inferiority of the Mosaic covenant and the transcendent excellence of the new and better covenant we find that the conception of covenant which we have already found is applied to the highest degree.   However accentuated may be the problem connected with the writer's evaluation of the Mosaic covenant, which he contrasts with the new, the resolution of this question will not interfere with our understanding of the conception he entertains respecting the new and better covenant.   It is a covenant with a more excellent ministry (Heb. viii. 6), that is to say, more excellent in respect of the access to God secured and the fellowship maintained.   To whatever extent the old covenant was the means of establishing the peculiar relation of the Lord to Israel as their God and their relation to Him as His people, the new covenant places this older intimacy of relation in the shadow.   For it is the new covenant *par excellence* which brings to realization the promise ' I will be to them a God, and they shall be to me a people ' (Heb. viii. 10).   In other words, the spiritual relationship which lay at the centre of the covenant grace disclosed in both the Abrahamic and Mosaic covenants reaches its ripest fruition in the new covenant.   So great is the enhancement that a comparative contrast can be stated as if it were absolute.   The new covenant is enacted upon better promises (Heb. viii. 6).   We found that bonded and oath-bound promise constitutes the essence of the covenant conception.   In the new covenant the promises are better and they are placed in the forefront as defining its superiority. Again, the new covenant is not indifferent to law. It is not contrasted with the old because the old had law and the new has not. The superiority of the new does not consist in the abrogation of that law but in its being brought into more intimate relation to us and more effective fulfilment in us. ' I will put my laws into their mind, and upon their hearts will I write them ' (Heb. viii. 10). The new covenant is the dispenser of the forgiveness of sins: ' I will be merciful to their unrighteousnesses, and their sins will I remember no more ' (Heb. viii. 12). Finally, the new covenant is one that universalizes the diffusion of knowledge: ' They shall all know me from the least unto the greatest of them ' (Heb. viii. 11). In all of this we have the covenant as a sovereign administration of grace and promise, constituting the relation of communion with God, coming to its richest and fullest expression. In a word, the new covenant is covenant as we have found it to be all along the line of redemptive revelation and accomplishment. But it is covenant in all these respects on the highest level of achievement. If the mark of covenant is divinity in initiation, administration, confirmation, and fulfilment, here we have divinity at the apex of its disclosure and activity.

(b) The concept of ' testament '

No instance of *diatheke* in the New Testament is more relevant to the thesis now being developed than Heb. ix. 16, 17. There have been interpreters who have taken the position that even in this passage the word should not be rendered or construed as testament but as covenant.[21] It seems to me that Geerhardus Vos has effectively dealt with the fallacy of this interpretation.[22] We

---

21 *Cf.* B. F. Westcott: *The Epistle to the Hebrews* (London, 1903), pp. 300ff.; David Russell: *A Familiar Survey of the Old and New Covenants* (Edinburgh, 1824), pp. 137ff.; Thomas Scott: *The New Testament of our Lord and Saviour Jesus Christ ad* Heb. ix. 16, 17. Scott is, however, not dogmatic. In reference to the interpretation which regards the death as that of the sacrifice rather than of the testator he says that he cannot but think that this is the most obvious and ' consonant to the apostle's general way of reasoning '.

22 See ' Hebrews, the Epistle of the Diatheke ' in *The Princeton Theological Review,* Vol. XIII, pp. 614ff.; *cf.* John Owen: *An Exposition of the Epistle to the Hebrews ad* Heb. ix. 16, 17.

may assume, therefore, that in these two verses the writer does introduce the testamentary notion of a last will. It is admittedly an exceptional use of the term as far as the New Testament is concerned,[23] and it is introduced for the specific purpose of illustrating the transcendent efficacy or effectiveness of the death of Christ in securing the benefits of covenant grace. Just as the disponement made in a last will goes into effect with the death of the testator and is thereupon of full force and validity for the benefit of the legatee, so, since Christ through the eternal Spirit offered Himself without spot to God, the blessing of the new covenant becomes ours. Specifically in terms of the context, our consciences are purged from dead works to serve the living God and we receive the promise of an eternal inheritance. The testamentary provisions referred to in verses 16 and 17 are introduced simply for the purpose of enforcing the efficacy of Jesus' death in bringing into effect the blessings of the new covenant. There is no more possibility or feasibility of interference with the effective application of the blessings of the covenant than there is of interfering with a testamentary disponement once the testator has died. This use of the testamentary provision of Roman law to illustrate the inviolable security accruing from the sacrificial death of Christ serves to underline the unilateral character of the new covenant. One thing is apparent that a testament is a unilateral disposition of possession. How totally foreign to the notion of compact, contract, or agreement is the disposition or dispensation which can be illustrated in respect of its effective operation by a last will! This occasional use of *diatheke* as testament cannot comport with a concept of covenant which in any way derives its definition from the idea of mutual agreement.

CONCLUSION

This brings to a close our review of the evidence bearing upon the nature of God's covenant with men. From the beginning of God's disclosures to men in terms of covenant we find a unity of

[23] It may well be that it is the testamentary idea that Paul uses in Gal. iii. 15. If so, it is obviously a last will or testament which could be regarded as immutably confirmed before the death of the testator, as in Syro-Grecian law, in contradistinction from that referred to in Heb. ix. 16, 17 which became operative with the death of the testator (*cf.* Vos: *op. cit.*, pp. 611ff.).

conception which is to the effect that a divine covenant is a sovereign administration of grace and of promise. It is not compact or contract or agreement that provides the constitutive or governing idea but that of dispensation in the sense of disposition. This central and basic concept is applied, however, to a variety of situations and the precise character of the grace bestowed and of the promise given differs in the differing covenant administrations. The differentiation does not reside in any deviation from this basic conception but simply consists in the differing degrees of richness and fulness of the grace bestowed and of the promise given. Preponderantly in the usage of Scripture covenant refers to grace and promise specifically redemptive. The successive covenants are coeval with the successive epochs in the unfolding and accomplishment of God's redemptive will. Not only are they coeval, they are correlative with these epochs. And not only are they correlative, they are themselves constitutive of these epochs so that redemptive revelation and accomplishment become identical with covenant revelation and accomplishment. When we appreciate this fact we come to perceive that the epochal strides in the unfolding of redemptive revelation are at the same time epochal advances in the disclosure of the riches of covenant grace. This progressive enrichment of the covenant grace bestowed is not, however, a retraction of or deviation from the concept which is constitutive from the beginning but, as we should expect, an expansion and intensification of it. Hence, when we come to the climax and apex of covenant administration in the New Testament epoch, we have sovereign grace and promise dispensed on the highest level because it is grace bestowed and promise given in regard to the attainment of the highest end conceivable for men. It is no wonder then that the new covenant is called the everlasting covenant. As covenant revelation has progressed throughout the ages it has reached its consummation in the new covenant and the new covenant is not wholly diverse in principle and character from the covenants which have preceded it and prepared for it but it is itself the complete realization and embodiment of that sovereign grace which was the constitutive principle of all the covenants. And when we remember that covenant is not only bestowment of grace, not only oath-bound promise, but also relationship with God in that which is the crown and goal of the whole process of religion, namely, union and communion with God, we discover again that the new covenant brings this relationship also to the highest level of achievement. At the centre of covenant revelation as its constant refrain is the assurance ' I will be your God, and ye shall be my people '. The new covenant does not differ from the earlier covenants because it inaugurates this peculiar intimacy. It differs simply because it brings to the ripest and richest fruition the relationship epitomized in that promise. In this respect also the new covenant is an everlasting covenant — there is no further expansion or enrichment. The mediator of the new covenant is none other than God's own Son, the effulgence of the Father's glory and the express image of His substance, the heir of all things. He is its surety also. And because there can be no higher mediator or surety than the Lord of glory, since there can be no sacrifice more transcendent in its efficacy and finality than the sacrifice of Him who through the eternal Spirit offered Himself without spot unto God, this covenant cannot give place to another. Grace and truth, promise and fulfilment, have in this covenant received their *pleroma,* and it is in terms of the new covenant that it will be said, ' Behold, the tabernacle of God is with men, and he will dwell with them, and they shall be his people, and God himself shall be with them ' (Rev. xxi. 3).